*Mundaka Upanishad
and Commentary*

By
Charles Johnston

Copyright © 2021 Lamp of Trismegistus. All rights reserved. No part of this publication may be reproduced or transmitted in any form or by any means, electronic or mechanical, including photocopying, recording, or by any information storage and retrieval system, without permission in writing from Lamp of Trismegistus. Reviewers may quote brief passages.

ISBN: 978-1-63118-496-3

Esoteric Classics:
Eastern Studies

Other Books in this Series and Related Titles

Isha Upanishad and Commentary by Charles Johnston (978-1-63118-490-1)

Kena Upanishad and Commentary by Charles Johnston (978-1-63118-491-8)

Katha Upanishad and Commentary by Charles Johnston (978-1-63118-493-2)

Prashna Upanishad and Commentary by Charles Johnston (978-1-63118-494-9)

Mandukya Upanishad and Commentary by Charles Johnston (978-1-63118-497-0)

Atma Bodha & Tattva Bodha by Adi Shankara &c (978-1-63118-401-7)

The Crest-Jewel of Wisdom by Adi Shankara (978-1-63118-475-8)

Catholicism, Yoga and Hinduism by Hartmann &c (978-1-63118-478-9)

Yoga, Hatha-Yoga and Raja-Yoga by Annie Besant (978-1-63118-476-5)

The Tree of Wisdom by Nagarjuna (978-1-63118-470-3)

The Path of Light: A Manual of Maha-Yana Buddhism (978-1-63118-471-0)

Buddhist Psalms by Shinran (978-1-63118-465-9)

Tao Te Ching & Commentary by Lao Tzu & C Johnston (978-1-63118-495-6)

The Hymns of Hermes by G. R. S. Mead (978-1-63118-405-5)

The Golden Verses of Pythagoras: Five Translations (978-1-63118-479-6)

Gnosis of the Mind by G. R. S. Mead (978-1-63118-408-6)

The Hymn of Jesus by G. R. S. Mead (978-1-63118-492-5)

The Book of the Watchers by Enoch (978-1-63118-416-1)

The Secrets of Enoch by Enoch (978-1-63118-449-9)

The Gospel of the Nativity of Mary by St. Matthew (978-1-63118-448-2)

A Collection of Early Writings on Astral Travel (978-1-63118-477-2)

Audio versions are also available on Audible, Amazon and Apple

Table of Contents

Introduction...7

Mundaka Upanishad
Translated by Charles Johnston...9

The Two Wisdoms
Commentary on the Mundaka Upanishad
By Charles Johnston...21

Moonduk Opunishud
Translated by Raja Ram Mohun Roy...45

INTRODUCTION

The word "esoteric" can be difficult to define. Esotericism in general can be seen less as a system of beliefs and more as a category, which encompasses numerous, different systems of beliefs. It's a bit of juxtaposition, since the word "esoteric" indicates something that few people know about, while the term itself broadly covers numerous philosophies, practices, areas of study and belief systems.

In a greater sense, Esotericism acts as a storehouse for secret knowledge, which is often considered ancient (*by tradition, if not by fact*), passed down from generation to generation, in private. At various times in history, simply possessing the knowledge of some of these subjects, was considered illegal and a jailable offence, if discovered. This usually included such general topics as Alchemy, Pharmacology, Qabalah, Hermeticism, Occultism, Ceremonial Magic, Astrology, Divination, Rosicrucianism and so on. Collectively, these areas of study were often referred to as the esoteric sciences.

Sometimes, the outer garment of a subject isn't esoteric, while what is hidden beneath it, is. As an example, Freemasonry isn't necessarily esoteric by nature (at *least not anymore*), but certain signs, passwords and handshakes given to the candidate during their initiation, are in fact, esoteric, in the sense that they are hidden from the general public.

Today, in the twenty-first century, such topics are readily available at bookstores across the country, and numerous mainsteam publishers offer beginners guides and coffee-table volumes on many of these subjects, intended for mass appeal. Books like *"The Secret"* have turned previously arcane topics into household knowledge. All that being the case, however, it isn't to say that there still aren't buried secrets to uncover, ancient wisdom being ignored and forgotten mysteries to be explored. In fact, it is often that we are only able to further our own studies by standing on the shoulders of these disappearing giants.

Lamp of Trismegistus is doing its part to help preserve humanity's esoteric history by making some of these classics available to those students who are seeking to unearth the knowledge of these ancient colossi.

So, be sure to check other titles from our *Esoteric Classics* series, as well as our *Occult Fiction, Theosophical Classics, Eastern Studies, Foundations of Freemasonry Series, Supernatural Fiction, Paranormal Research Series, Studies in Buddhism* and our *Christian Apocrypha Series.* You can also download the audio versions of most of these titles from Amazon, Apple or Audible, for learning on the go.

MUNDAKA UPANISHAD

Translated by Charles Johnston

Brahmâ the Evolver, first of the Bright Powers came to birth, Maker of all, Preserver of the world. He declared the Wisdom of the Eternal, the root and foundation of all wisdom, to Atharvan, his eldest son. The Wisdom of the Eternal which Brahmâ imparted to Atharvan, that of old Atharvan declared to Angir. Angir declared it to Satyavaha of the line of Bharadvaja. The descendant of Bharadvaja declared it to Angiras, both the higher and the lower wisdom.

Shaunaka, verily, lord of a great dwelling, coming according to rule to Angiras, asked him: Master through the knowledge of what does all this become known?

To him he said: Two wisdoms are to be known, as the knowers of the Eternal declare, the higher and the lower wisdom.

The lower wisdom is, the Rig Veda, Yajur Veda, Sama Veda, Atharva Veda, Pronunciation, Ritual, Grammar, Definition, Metres and Knowledge of the stars.

So the higher wisdom is that whereby the Everlasting is attained.

That which is invisible, intangible, without family or colour, without sight or hearing, without hands or feet; eternal, all-pervading, omnipresent, most subtle, that imperishable which the wise behold as the source of beings.

As the spider puts forth and draws in the thread; as plants come to birth upon the earth; as hair and down grow on a living man; so from that Everlasting the whole world comes to birth.

Through fervour and penance the Eternal is gained. From the Eternal, food comes to birth. From food, the life-breath, mind, truth, the worlds, and the immortal in works.

He who is all-knowing, all-wise, whose fervour and penance consist in wisdom, through him this Eternal, and name and form, and food come to birth.

There is this truth:

The works which the Seers beheld in the chants are set forth manifold in the three Vedas.

Perform them faithfully, ye who desire the truth; this is your path to the world of reward.

When the tongued flame quivers, after the fire of oblations has been kindled, then between the two portions of consecrated oil let him throw the oblations.

He who follows not the Agnihotra sacrifice with the sacrifice of the new moon and full moon, the four months sacrifice and the harvest sacrifice; he who invites not guests to the sacrifice, or offers no sacrifice, or a sacrifice without summoning all the gods, or without due rites, such a one loses the seven worlds.

These are the seven quivering tongues of flame: the black, the terrible, the mind-swift, the ruddy, the dark red, the sparkling and the glowing brilliant.

If he perform sacrifice while these are glowing, offering the oblations at the right time, these as sun rays lead him to the dwelling of the lord of the gods.

Calling, Come! Come! the shining oblations carry the sacrificer with the sun's rays, speaking fair words and praising; This is your holy Heaven, your world of reward!

Infirm boats are these forms of sacrifice, the eighteen, in which are set forth the lower work. Those who, deluded, think this the better way, go again to decay and death.

Others, turning about in the unwisdom of delusion, self-wise, thinking themselves learned, stray, wandering in the way, deluded, like the blind led by the blind.

Turning about in manifold unwisdom, foolishly thinking, We have done the work! the followers of ritual perceive not because of their desires. Therefore, when their world of reward fails, they fall in misery.

Thinking the merit of burnt offerings is best, they are deluded, not perceiving the other and better way. After they have received their reward in the paradise gained by their works, they return to this, or, perchance, a lower world.

But they who follow after fervour and faith, who in the forest dwell in peace, wise, serving the Eternal, purified from passion, they pass through the door of the Sun, to the Immortal, the Spirit, the imperishable Soul.

Discerning the worlds that are won by these works, let him renounce them. The uncreated is not won by works like these. In order that he may gain knowledge of these things, let him approach the Master, with kindling wood in his hands; a Master full of spiritual wisdom, firmly established in the Eternal. To the disciple who has thus drawn near to him, whose turbulent thoughts have been stilled, who has entered into peace, the wise Master teaches that truth whereby he knows the imperishable Spirit, the wisdom of the Eternal in its reality.

There is this truth:

As from a blazing fire sparks come forth a thousandfold, of like nature to it; so, beloved, from the Everlasting are born manifold beings, and thither also they return.

For divine, without form, is Spirit; He is without and within, unborn; without breath or mind, pure, above the highest imperishable Nature.

From Him are born life-breath and mind and all the powers that perceive and act, the aether, air, fire, the waters, and earth, the bearer of all.

The Fire-god is His head, His eyes are sun and moon; the spaces are His ears; revealed wisdom is His voice; the air is His life-breath, the world is His heart, from His feet comes the earth; for He is the Inmost Soul of all beings.

From Him comes the fire whose fuel is the sun; from the moon-power comes rain, and plants spring up on the earth. Spirit sends forth energy into Nature; through Spirit, many beings come to birth.

From Him come the chants of the Rig Veda, the Sama and Yajur Vedas initiatory rites, all sacrifices, ceremonies, gifts; the circling year also, the sacrificer, the world where the moon shines and the world illumined by the sun.

From Him also the divinities in their many forms received being, and the seraphs and men and beasts and birds; from Him the forward life and the downward life; from Him rice and barley; from Him, fervour and faith and truth, service of the Eternal and the disciple's rule.

From Him come forth the seven lives; from Him the seven flames and their several fuel; from Him come the seven offerings. Seven are these worlds wherein the seven lives gain their experience, hidden in the secret place, according to seven and seven.

From Him come the oceans and all hills; from Him the rivers flow in their many forms; from Him come all plants, and the fine essence through which the Inner Soul stands in beings.

For that Spirit is all that is: work, fervour, the Eternal, the supreme immortal. He who knows this Spirit hidden in the inner being, he, beloved, unties the knot of the heart.

The Eternal is manifest, yet concealed; Moving-in-secret is its name; it is the great abode in which all things are set firm.

It moves and breathes, with opening and closing eyes; know ye that this, which is Being and non-being, is to be sought after; it is beyond the understanding of creatures, it is most excellent. It is fiery, more subtile than the atom; in it these worlds are set, and the dwellers in the worlds.

This is the enduring Eternal, this is Life, the Word, Mind. This is the Truth, this, the Immortal. This is to be aimed at as the mark; pierce that mark, beloved!

Grasping the potent weapon, the Secret Wisdom, as thy bow, fit to it the arrow of thought sharpened by meditation, drawing the bow with the heart filled with the Being of That, aim at the Everlasting as thy mark, beloved!

The holy syllable is the bow; the arrow is thyself; the Eternal is the mark. The arrow should be sped by him who has conquered delusion; let him find lodgment in That, as the arrow in the mark.

That whereon Heaven and Earth and the space between are woven, with Mind and all lives; know ye That as the One, without other names, for That is the bridge of immortality.

As spokes are set in the nave of the wheel, in Him are the life-courses set; through them He moves in manifold forms of life. Meditate ye on the Soul through the holy syllable; may it be well with you, in crossing to the shore beyond the darkness.

He who is all-knowing, all-wise, whose is this greatness in the world, He is the Soul, established in the city of the Eternal, in the heavenly ether.

Formed of mind, leader of life and of the body, established in food, dwelling in the heart, Him the wise discern through wisdom, formed of joy, immortal, radiant.

The knot of the heart is untied, all doubts are cut; his bondage through works wears out, when That is known, which is above and below.

In the highest golden vesture is the stainless, partless Eternal: that radiant One, the light of lights, whom the knowers of the Soul know.

The sun shines not there, nor the moon and stars, nor these lightnings, nor fire like this; after the shining of this, all things shine; by the light of this, all else is illumined.

The Eternal, verily, is this, immortal; the Eternal is before, the Eternal is behind, the Eternal is on the right hand, the Eternal is on the left; extended below and above is the Eternal, the Eternal is all this, to the uttermost.

Two birds, close comrades, rest on the same tree. One of them eats the sweet fruit; the other watches, eating not.

In that tree is man, sunk down, grieving for his lost power, deluded; when he sees the other, the Lord in his greatness, as one with him, he is freed from sorrow.

When the seer beholds the Maker, the spiritual man, bearing within him the Eternal, then, illumined by wisdom, passing beyond both works enjoined and works forbidden, stainless, he attains to supreme oneness.

This is the Life that shines through all beings; knowing Him, he attains to wisdom, for there is no other who imparts wisdom. Rejoicing in the Soul, delighting in the Soul, accomplishing all things, he becomes the most excellent knower of the Eternal.

For this Soul is to be gained by truth, by fervour, by thorough knowledge, by service of the Eternal perpetually rendered.

In the body within, formed of light and radiant is he, whom they who strive toward him behold, they whose sins are worn away.

Truth conquers, and not untruth; by truth is the path, the divine way, ascended, the path by which the seers go, who have gained their desire, to the supreme treasure house of truth.

Great is that, divine, in form beyond thought, more subtile than the subtile, shining forth. Farther than far, yet it is close at hand; here, hidden in the heart, for those who have vision.

Not by the eye is that apprehended, not by speech, nor by the other powers, nor by penance and the works of the law; through the grace of wisdom, when the heart is pure, through meditation he beholds Him who is undivided.

This subtile Soul is to be known through the heart, into which life has entered fivefold; through these life-forces the whole consciousness of beings is woven; when this consciousness is purified, the Soul shines forth.

Whatever world he who is purified conceives in his heart, whatever desires he desires, that world he wins, and those desires; therefore let him who seeks well-being honour him who knows the Soul.

He knows the supreme dwelling of the Eternal, resting in which the world shines, luminous. They who have conquered their desires, draw near to the spiritual man; full of wisdom, they conquer the seed of rebirth in the world.

He who desires desires, dwelling on them in his mind, through these desires he is reborn in this place or in that. But he who has attained his desire, who has gained the Soul, from him even in this world all desires melt away.

Not by speaking is the Soul gained, nor by much reasoning, nor by hearing much; whom the Soul chooses, by him it is gained; the Soul reveals its own form to him.

Nor is the Soul to be attained by him who lacks valour, nor by the heedless, nor by penance without renunciation. But when he wisely strives through the right means, this Soul enters his heart, where dwells the Eternal.

Attaining Him, rejoicing in wisdom, purified from passion, gaining peace, winning that all-penetrating Soul, wise, united with the Soul, the seers enter into the All.

They who have understood that wisdom which is the essence of the Vedas, who strive through renunciation and union, purified in heart, all these at the time of the end gain liberation, immortal in the realm of the Eternal.

Gone are the thrice five parts in their places, and all the shining powers in their several shining, and all works, and the self of mental action; all have become one in the unchanging Supreme.

As rivers, flowing to the ocean, go to their setting, putting off name and form, so the possessor of wisdom, freed from name and form, gains that Spirit which is higher than the highest, the Divine.

He who knows the supreme Eternal, becomes the Eternal, nor is any born in his line who knows not the Eternal. He crosses beyond sorrow, he crosses beyond sin, freed from the knots of the heart he becomes immortal.

This is declared by the Vedic verse:

They who fulfil the rites, who hear the Vedas, who are established in the Eternal, who offer themselves with faith in the one Seer; to them let him declare wisdom, who have duly fulfilled the head vow.

This is the truth which the seer Angiras declared of old. He receives it not, who has not fulfilled the vow.

Obeisance to the supreme Seers!

Obeisance to the supreme Seers!

THE TWO WISDOMS

MUNDAKA Upanishad

Translated from the Sanskrit with an Interpretation

By Charles Johnston

Brahmâ the Evolver, first of the Bright Powers came to birth, Maker of all, Preserver of the world. He declared the Wisdom of the Eternal, the root and foundation of all wisdom, to Atharvan, his eldest son. The Wisdom of the Eternal which Brahmâ imparted to Atharvan, that of old Atharvan declared to Angir. Angir declared it to Satyavaha of the line of Bharadvaja. The descendant of Bharadvaja declared it to Angiras, both the higher and the lower wisdom.

Brahmâ is the manifest Logos, the Logos as Creator, or, more truly, as Evolver, since the Substance of Being is beginningless. The "coming to birth" of Brahmâ is the manifestation of the Creative Logos from the first, the unmanifest Logos. Brahmâ is, therefore, Avalokita-Ishvara, the Lord made manifest, the Host of the Divine Powers regarded as a unity.

The thought here is that Divine Wisdom was revealed, at the beginning of this world-period, to a chosen nucleus of humanity, and that it has ever since been handed down from Master to disciple, in unbroken succession.

In the Vedas it is said that Atharvan was a kinsman and companion of the Divine Powers, the first to bring down fire from Heaven and to impart to mankind the draught of Soma, which brings illumination. We may, therefore, see in him the incarnate Planetary Spirit who imparted Divine Wisdom to primitive mankind. Angir does not appear to be mentioned except in the passage translated above. Satyavaha means Bearer of Truth. Angiras is connected by some philologists with the Greek Angelos, a Messenger between Gods and men; the Angirases, taken collectively, are Sons of the Gods and Fathers of mankind. They are compared by philologists with the Sons of God in the sixth chapter of Genesis. They were the first to ascend into Heaven and win immortality.

This introductory passage, therefore, would seem to point to the origin and indicate the powers of the Lodge of Masters, as Sons of the Divine Powers and spiritual Fathers of mankind.

Shaunaka, verily, lord of a great dwelling, coming according to rule to Angiras, asked him: Master through the knowledge of what does all this become known?

To him he said: Two wisdoms are to be known, as the knowers of the Eternal declare, the higher and the lower wisdom.

The lower wisdom is, the Rig Veda, Yajur Veda, Sama Veda, Atharva Veda, Pronunciation, Ritual, Grammar, Definition, Metres and Knowledge of the stars.

So the higher wisdom is that whereby the Everlasting is attained.

That which is invisible, intangible, without family or colour, without sight or hearing, without hands or feet; eternal, all-pervading, omnipresent, most subtile, that imperishable which the wise behold as the source of beings.

As the spider puts forth and draws in the thread; as plants come to birth upon the earth; as hair and down grow on a living man; so from that Everlasting the whole world comes to birth.

Through fervour and penance the Eternal is gained. From the Eternal, food comes to birth. From food, the life-breath, mind, truth, the worlds, and the immortal in works.

He who is all-knowing, all-wise, whose fervour and penance consist in wisdom, through him this Eternal, and name and form, and food come to birth.

As is so often the case in the Upanishads, the teaching is introduced in the form of communion between a Master and his pupil, as though to remind us that only in this way is real wisdom gained. Shaunaka, we are told, came to Angiras as a pupil, according to rule: that is, with the heart and will of a disciple. The Master replies that there are two kinds of wisdom, the lower and the higher.

The lower includes the whole range of knowledge possessed by ancient India: The four Vedas, and the six subsidiary studies which lead to the full understanding of the Vedas. It should be understood that the Vedas are not thought of as so many poems, or even as so many hymns. They are really magical instruments, the means whereby the student of the Vedas hopes to command supernatural powers. Perhaps it will be more intelligible if we say that they were thought of as the means for entering and gaining command over the whole astral world. But the Master puts all this aside as the lower wisdom. The higher wisdom is that whereby the spiritual and Divine is gained.

Then comes the definition of the Eternal by negatives, the purpose being, first, to lead the disciple's understanding beyond the anthropomorphism of the popular gods, and then to awaken his spiritual vision of that Divine Being from which all manifested beings come forth, and to which they are all destined to return.

Not through gifts and offerings, but through fervour and purification is gained the consciousness of the Eternal, that Being whence comes the food of all beings; both their sustenance and their experience, which is the food of life. Therefore consecrated food symbolizes experience of divine things. And through the sustenance which we draw day by day from the Eternal, comes the breath of life in us, our conscious existence; from the Eternal comes the conscious mind, with its power of discerning truth; from the Eternal comes the power to enter into the many mansions of the spiritual world; from the Eternal comes the power to build the house not made with hands, eternal in the heavens; to build that life whose works are immortal.

From the Eternal, in the cosmic sense, all things come forth, all worlds, all life-energies, all consciousness. And, in the more individual sense, through the intuition and spiritual perception of the Eternal comes the building up of an enduring nature in man, with access to higher worlds and a deeper vision of truth.

The last sentence translated above appears to mean this: Through the aid of the Master, all-knowing, all-wise, the knowledge of the Eternal comes to birth in the disciple, with name and form, implying true individuality, and that daily food for the inner nature which comes through the Master's grace and help.

Then follows a passage which dramatically sets forth the substance of the Vedic sacrificial system, the body of the lower wisdom, as it might appear to one of its devotees. And this is immediately followed by a condemnation of that system and the exaltation of the higher wisdom. It is exactly the antithesis which has been brought out before, between the Path of the Sun, which leads to liberation, and the Path of the Moon, which leads back again to this world through the bondage of Karma. We come first to the dramatic presentation of the lower wisdom.

There is this truth:

The works which the Seers beheld in the chants are set forth manifold in the three Vedas.

Perform them faithfully, ye who desire the truth; this is your path to the world of reward.

When the tongued flame quivers, after the fire of oblations has been kindled, then between the two portions of consecrated oil let him throw the oblations.

He who follows not the Agnihotra sacrifice with the sacrifice of the new moon and full moon, the four months sacrifice and the harvest sacrifice; he who invites not guests to the sacrifice, or offers no sacrifice, or a sacrifice without summoning all the gods, or without due rites, such a one loses the seven worlds.

These are the seven quivering tongues of flame: the black, the terrible, the mind-swift, the ruddy, the dark red, the sparkling and the glowing brilliant.

If he perform sacrifice while these are glowing, offering the oblations at the right time, these as sun rays lead him to the dwelling of the lord of the gods.

Calling, Come! Come! the shining oblations carry the sacrificer with the sun's rays, speaking fair words and praising; This is your holy Heaven, your world of reward!

So far, the dramatic picture of the system of fire-sacrifices. But there always lingers the thought that these Vedic ceremonies had once, perhaps in a far earlier day, a deeper and higher meaning; that this deeper meaning was veiled and obscured when the Brahmans turned the ancient Vedic system into a ceremonial religion, to rivet the power of their priestcraft upon India. There is, perhaps, the suggestion of seven modes of electrical force in the names of the seven tongues of fire. But the evident intention here is to condemn the ritual way to the paradise of selfish rewards, as the following passage shows.

It may be explained in advance that "the eighteen" are the four Vedas, each divided into three parts, and thus together making twelve, to which are added the six subsidiary studies already enumerated.

Infirm boats are these forms of sacrifice, the eighteen, in which are set forth the lower work. Those who, deluded, think this the better way, go again to decay and death.

Others, turning about in the unwisdom of delusion, self-wise, thinking themselves learned, stray, wandering in the way, deluded, like the blind led by the blind.

Turning about in manifold unwisdom, foolishly thinking, We have done the work! the followers of ritual perceive not because of their desires. Therefore, when their world of reward fails, they fall in misery.

Thinking the merit of burnt offerings is best, they are deluded, not perceiving the other and better way. After they have received their reward in the paradise gained by their works, they return to this, or, perchance, a lower world.

But they who follow after fervour and faith, who in the forest dwell in peace, wise, serving the Eternal, purified from passion, they pass through the door of the Sun, to the Immortal, the Spirit, the imperishable Soul.

We may tell ourselves that we are not likely to offer burnt offerings, or to strew oblations in the flames, or to chant the Vedic hymns. We may also, perhaps, congratulate ourselves that we are not working for their paradise of rewards. Therefore all these things may seem remote and almost meaningless to us.

But we should realize that any act whatever, done in order that we ourselves may gain a reward of relished sensation or flattered vanity, is a burnt offering to a false god. There are more ways than one of making a Vedic sacrifice, and many of them we practise daily. When we make oblations to our desires, when we contrive and work to win flattery from ourselves and others, when we are wrapt in self, we are devotees of the ritual system that is here condemned. Not only the fire on the altar, but also the life-fires within ourselves, all our energies and powers, can be turned to evil self-seeking. Every impulse of sloth, every shirking of effort, is the seeking of a paradise of reward and repose, from which we shall sink miserably to a lower state.

In contrast with those who practise the rites of self-seeking oblations, the closing lines of this passage describe the followers of the higher way. There is a literal and a symbolic meaning. First, the life of disciples, in well guarded seclusion in the forest or among the mountains, inspired by fiery aspiration and faith, dwelling in quietude of heart, seeking wisdom, serving in the purity of life that has seen and turned from the evil of passionate desires. But there is also the deeper and more universal meaning. The word translated "forest" means also wilderness, desert; it is a description of this whole material world, which is a wilderness in comparison with the spiritual world. We are dwelling in the wilderness, and those are the energies which we should exercise, if we would pass from self through the door of the Sun to selflessness. This would seem to be the same symbol as the Gates of Gold.

Discerning the worlds that are won by these works, let him renounce them. The uncreated is not won by works like these. In order that he may gain knowledge of these things, let him approach the Master, with kindling wood in his hands; a Master full of spiritual wisdom, firmly established in the Eternal. To the disciple who has thus drawn near to him, whose turbulent thoughts have been stilled, who has entered into peace, the wise Master teaches that truth whereby he knows the imperishable Spirit, the wisdom of the Eternal in its reality.

The word rendered "renounce" means more than this. It implies a nauseated revulsion and at the same time a completely realized indifference, to be gained as the fruit of revulsion. The commentary attributed to Shankaracharya says that we discern the true nature of the world of self-indulgence as the traveller in the desert discerns the true nature of the lake conjured up by mirage; and, seeing through the glamour, we turn from delusion to seek reality. Then it is possible to find the Master. The disciple brings kindling wood, the power to be enkindled. The Master communicates to him the divine fire of selfless aspiration.

There is this truth:

As from a blazing fire sparks come forth a thousandfold, of like nature to it; so, beloved, from the Everlasting are born manifold beings, and thither also they return.

For divine, without form, is Spirit; He is without and within, unborn; without breath or mind, pure, above the highest imperishable Nature.

From Him are born life-breath and mind and all the powers that perceive and act, the aether, air, fire, the waters, and earth, the bearer of all.

The Fire-god is His head, His eyes are sun and moon; the spaces are His ears; revealed wisdom is His voice; the air is His life-breath, the world is His heart, from His feet comes the earth; for He is the Inmost Soul of all beings.

From Him comes the fire whose fuel is the sun; from the moon-power comes rain, and plants spring up on the earth. Spirit sends forth energy into Nature; through Spirit, many beings come to birth.

From Him come the chants of the Rig Veda, the Sama and Yajur Vedas initiatory rites, all sacrifices, ceremonies, gifts; the circling year also, the sacrificer, the world where the moon shines and the world illumined by the sun.

The effort of the Master here is, to awaken in the disciple the understanding and intuition of the Logos, that primal Life which is manifested in every form of life. These lives appear to come forth; in reality they remain in and of the Logos. Therefore, however dire may be our imprisonment, the Divine Power is there also, in touch with us, ready to help and liberate us, the instant we sincerely desire to be rid of our bonds. We are the kindred sparks that have come forth from the great Light.

Spirit is without form, yet all forms have their origin in Spirit. Spirit is unborn, and yet is the source of all beings that come to birth. Spirit is without personal, limited life-breath or mind; yet all life and all mind derive directly from Spirit. All things are within this great Life, and the Life is in all things; therefore Spirit is within and without. Nature, the power of manifestation, is everlasting. There is the eternal dual potency in Parabrahm: Spirit and Nature; Subjective and Objective; Noumenal and Phenomenal. But the noumenal, the perceiving consciousness, is always more fundamental than the thing perceived. Spirit is, therefore, higher than Nature.

The Logos is the source at once of all our inner powers, consciousness and perception and will, and of the outer powers and elements which make up the visible worlds. And the Master uses vivid symbols to lead the disciple to recognize the Logos in all the world about him: the celestial fire which gives life to the universe is His head; sun and moon are His eyes; the expanse of space is his power of hearing; the air is His life-breath; the world is His heart. Every sentence and symbol should be pondered over and imaginatively realized, until, like that disciple, we recognize the immanent Spirit in all things, and learn to find His voice in the words of all scriptures. We may understand the world where the moon shines as the astral world; the world illumined by the sun is the spiritual.

From Him also the divinities in their many forms received being, and the seraphs and men and beasts and birds; from Him the forward-life and the downward-life; from Him rice and barley; from Him, fervour and faith and truth, service of the Eternal and the disciple's rule.

From Him come forth the seven lives; from Him the seven flames and their several fuel; from Him come the seven offerings. Seven are these worlds wherein the seven lives gain their experience, hidden in the secret place, according to seven and seven.

From Him come the oceans and all hills; from Him the rivers flow in their many forms; from Him come all plants, and the fine essence through which the Inner Soul stands in beings.

For that Spirit is all that is: work, fervour, the Eternal, the supreme immortal. He who knows this Spirit hidden in the inner being, he, beloved, unties the knot of the heart.

The Master continues the teaching of the Logos, which is set forth with such simple, vivid beauty, that comment is almost superfluous. Two sentences, perhaps, may be made a little clearer. The fine essence through which the Inner Soul stands in beings appears to be subtile substance from which is woven the vesture of consciousness, first in the natural body, and, after that, the vestures of the psychical and spiritual bodies. Atma, which is without individuality, receives individuality through these vestures. The knot of the heart is egotism, the great delusion of separateness. This sense of separate being is at first the incentive of our life and effort; later, becoming an intolerable burden, it becomes the incentive that drives us toward selflessness, to escape from the haunting obsession of self.

The Eternal is manifest, yet concealed; Moving-in-secret is its name; it is the great abode in which all things are set firm.

It moves and breathes, with opening and closing eyes; know ye that this, which is Being and non-being, is to be sought after; it is beyond the understanding of creatures, it is most excellent. It is fiery, more subtile than the atom; in it these worlds are set, and the dwellers in the worlds.

This is the enduring Eternal, this is Life, the Word, Mind. This is the Truth, this, the Immortal. This is to be aimed at as the mark; pierce that mark, beloved!

Grasping the potent weapon, the Secret Wisdom, as thy bow, fit to it the arrow of thought sharpened by meditation, drawing the bow with the heart filled with the Being of That, aim at the Everlasting as thy mark, beloved!

The holy syllable is the bow; the arrow is thyself; the Eternal is the mark. The arrow should be sped by him who has conquered delusion; let him find lodgment in That, as the arrow in the mark.

That whereon Heaven and Earth and the space between are woven, with Mind and all lives; know ye That as the One, without other names, for That is the bridge of immortality.

As spokes are set in the nave of the wheel, in Him are the life-courses set; through them He moves in manifold forms of life. Meditate ye on the Soul through the holy syllable; may it be well with you, in crossing to the shore beyond the darkness.

The Eternal is manifest in the whole manifest universe, yet concealed as to its own unknowable Being. Moving-in-secret is its name, because it is the hidden motive force, the inner driving power, in everything from the atom to the cosmos. We find ourselves steady in the midst of space; wherever we are, it is always "here"; we are thus steadfast because our inmost being rests, set firm in the Eternal.

We have the same contrast which Plato draws, between the Eternal, which ever is, but never becomes, and the manifested worlds, which never are, in the sense of final reality, though they are ever becoming. In this sense, the Eternal is both Being and non-being. And what a superb picture of the Eternal, alternately manifest in Manvantara and concealed in Pralaya: "It moves and breathes, with opening and closing eyes."

The Commentary attributed to Shankaracharya contains a passage of exceptional eloquence, referring to these verses: "Who is that Mighty One? It is He, at whose command Heaven and Earth stand apart, separated from each other; He, at whose command sun and moon move for ever, glowing like whirled firebrands; He, at whose command the rivers and the oceans transgress not their bounds; He, at whose command all things that move or move not are established; He, at whose command the seasons and the waters trespass not; He is the Mighty One."

The full meaning of the holy syllable, Om, is set forth at length in *Mandukya Upanishad*, to be translated next in this series. As regards the macrocosm, it symbolizes the three worlds, earth, interspace, heaven, summed up in the divine world which contains them all; as regards the microcosm, it symbolizes the three worlds in man, in their ascending order: the natural man, the psychical man, the spiritual man, consummated in the divine man; or it is the consciousness of each of these, again in ascending order. And the ascent from the ordinary consciousness of the natural man, to the supreme consciousness of the divine man, through meditation enkindled by fiery aspiration, is symbolized in the Upanishad by the arrow shot at the mark, and lodging in the mark.

He who is under delusion looks not toward the Eternal, but toward broken reflections of the Eternal in visible, material things, by which his eyes are fascinated. He must break this fascination through his ardent desire for Truth, before he can begin to aim at the Eternal.

The concept of the remaining verses is almost exactly that of Dante, in the twenty-seventh Canto of the *Paradiso*:

"The nature of the universe which stilleth the centre and moveth all the rest around, hence doth begin as from its starting point. And this heaven hath no other 'where' than the Divine Mind wherein is enkindled the love which revolveth it and the power which it poureth forth like rain. Light and love grasp it in one circle, as doth it the others, and this engirdment He only who doth gird it understandeth. Its movement by no other is marked out; but by it all the rest are measured."

He who is all-knowing, all-wise, whose is this greatness in the world, He is the Soul, established in the city of the Eternal, in the heavenly ether.

Formed of mind, leader of life and of the body, established in food, dwelling in the heart, Him the wise discern through wisdom, formed of joy, immortal, radiant.

The knot of the heart is untied, all doubts are cut; his bondage through works wears out, when That is known, which is above and below.

In the highest golden vesture is the stainless, partless Eternal: that radiant One, the light of lights, whom the knowers of the Soul know.

The sun shines not there, nor the moon and stars, nor these lightnings, nor fire like this; after the shining of this, all things shine; by the light of this, all else is illumined.

The Eternal, verily, is this, immortal; the Eternal is before, the Eternal is behind, the Eternal is on the right hand, the Eternal is on the left; extended below and above is the Eternal, the Eternal is all this, to the uttermost.

When the disciple, through the use of intellect and intuition, has gained some conception of the Eternal as the Life of all things, he is bidden to seek that Eternal within his own heart, superbly called "the city of the Eternal": "For within you is the light of the world—the only light that can be shed upon the Path. If you are unable to perceive it within you, it is useless to look for it elsewhere. It is beyond you; because when you reach it you have lost yourself. It is unattainable, because it for ever recedes. You will enter the light, but you will never touch the flame."

The Soul is the leader of life and of the body, because by the Soul the whole setting of life and every event are ordained, for the purpose of the Soul; the powers of the body are the outer manifestation of the powers of the Soul, made concrete in order that the earlier steps of experience may be more easily gained. It is established in food, because food is the symbol of experience, which is the food of character, the food by which the inner life grows.

The knot of the heart is the sense of separateness. The disciple "grasps his whole individuality firmly, and by force of his awakened spiritual will recognizes this individuality as not himself, but that thing which he has with pain created for his own use, and by means of which he purposes, as his growth slowly develops his intelligence, to reach to the life beyond individuality. When he knows that for this his wonderful complex separated life exists, then, indeed, and then only, he is upon the way."

The symbol of the Eternal as the light of lights is as old, perhaps, as the soul of man, as old as light itself. It runs through all the Scriptures of the world. Isaiah uses the same simile: "The sun shall be no more thy light by day; neither for brightness shall the moon give light unto thee; but the Lord shall be unto thee an everlasting light, and thy God thy glory." An even closer parallel is found in the *Revelation*: "And the city had no need of the sun, neither of the moon, to shine in it: for the glory of God did lighten it, and the Lamb is the light thereof."

Two birds, close comrades, rest on the same tree. One of them eats the sweet fruit; the other watches, eating not.

In that tree is man, sunk down, grieving for his lost power, deluded; when he sees the other, the Lord in his greatness, as one with him, he is freed from sorrow.

When the seer beholds the Maker, the spiritual man, bearing within him the Eternal, then, illumined by wisdom, passing beyond both works enjoined and works forbidden, stainless, he attains to supreme oneness.

This is the Life that shines through all beings; knowing Him, he attains to wisdom, for there is no other who imparts wisdom. Rejoicing in the Soul, delighting in the Soul, accomplishing all things, he becomes the most excellent knower of the Eternal.

The parable of the two birds joined together in close companionship indicates the relation of the inner and the outer self. The inner self watches, while the outer self eats the fruit of the tree of life. The outer self is man, sunk down, grieving for his lost power, deluded; when he regains the vision of the inner self, the Lord in his greatness, as being his true self, then he is freed from sorrow.

This would seem to be that stage on the way, of which it is said: "Look for the warrior and let him fight in thee. Take his orders for battle and obey them. Obey him not as though he were a general, but as though he were thyself, and his spoken words were the utterance of thy secret desires; for he is thyself, yet infinitely wiser and stronger than thyself."

For this Soul is to be gained by truth, by fervour, by thorough knowledge, by service of the Eternal perpetually rendered.

In the body within, formed of light and radiant is he, whom they who strive toward him behold, they whose sins are worn away.

Truth conquers, and not untruth; by truth is the path, the divine way, ascended, the path by which the seers go, who have gained their desire, to the supreme treasure house of truth.

Great is that, divine, in form beyond thought, more subtile than the subtile, shining forth. Farther than far, yet it is close at hand; here, hidden in the heart, for those who have vision.

Not by the eye is that apprehended, not by speech, nor by the other powers, nor by penance and the works of the law; through the grace of wisdom, when the heart is pure, through meditation he beholds Him who is undivided.

This subtile Soul is to be known through the heart, into which life has entered fivefold; through these life-forces the whole consciousness of beings is woven; when this consciousness is purified, the Soul shines forth.

Whatever world he who is purified conceives in his heart, whatever desires he desires, that world he wins, and those desires; therefore let him who seeks well-being honour him who knows the Soul.

The Soul is to be gained by truth. If we consider that the Eternal is made manifest to us in truth, beauty and goodness, we shall, perhaps, find it to be true that our own age has a deeper reverence for truth than for either goodness or beauty. Those who devote their lives to the search for truth, in the many fields of science, would appear to be more convinced, more in earnest, more whole hearted in their search than, let us say, the devotees of art, poetry, painting, who are professed seekers of beauty; or than those who make a profession of the search for goodness, in religion. These are sincere in their way, but they seem in a sense to lack both the high enthusiasm for truth which inspires so many followers of science, and the final determination to follow the truth, to seek the truth, to pay any price for the truth, which so many men of science have. The men of science willingly undertake greater sacrifices, and, just because of their deep reverence for truth, and their profound determination to attain to truth, they do not think of their undertakings in terms of sacrifice, but rather in terms of promise, of opportunity. This profound reverence for truth, this indomitable determination to pay any price whatever to attain it, counting that price a splendid opportunity, is the spirit which must inspire the disciple, who must likewise have the same disinterested and impersonal worship of truth for its own sake.

He knows the supreme dwelling of the Eternal, resting in which the world shines, luminous. They who have conquered their desires, draw near to the spiritual man; full of wisdom, they conquer the seed of rebirth in the world.

He who desires desires, dwelling on them in his mind, through these desires he is reborn in this place or in that. But he who has attained his desire, who has gained the Soul, from him even in this world all desires melt away.

Not by speaking is the Soul gained, nor by much reasoning, nor by hearing much; whom the Soul chooses, by him it is gained; the Soul reveals its own form to him.

Nor is the Soul to be attained by him who lacks valour, nor by the heedless, nor by penance without renunciation. But when he wisely strives through the right means, this Soul enters his heart, where dwells the Eternal.

Attaining Him, rejoicing in wisdom, purified from passion, gaining peace, winning that all-penetrating Soul, wise, united with the Soul, the seers enter into the All.

This passage is so full of the simplicity of beauty that it hardly needs any comment. But there is, perhaps, one phrase on which further light may be shed by a comparison with other Scriptures: "Whom the Soul chooses, by him it is gained."

Take the words of the Western Master: "Ye have not chosen me, but I have chosen you, and ordained you"; or the words of his heroic disciple, Paul: "When it pleased God, who separated me from my mother's womb, and called me by his grace, to reveal his Son in me ..." and think of the endless speculations concerning predestination and foreordination which have been based on them, causing on the one hand much spiritual pride and vanity, and on the other, deep moral anguish;

and it becomes apparent how great is the need of wisdom and of humility, in interpreting passages like these.

It would seem to be a question of perspective, of seeing the Soul, the Higher Self, in its true relation to the lower, personal self; the whole series of personal lives existing for the purposes of the Soul, that the divine powers of the Soul may be brought forth and made manifest. If we see this, then we can think of the Soul planning, guiding, supervising the whole series of lives; in these lives developing, one after another, its divine potentialities into actualities; and finally, when the time is ripe, summoning the personal self to become one with its divine prototype, so that the full essence of individual life, which has been brought to a focus through personal experience, may be carried over into the Soul. In that given life, then, when maturity had been reached, the Soul might be said to choose the personal man; to this extent, predestination would be a reality. But it is evident that the power of the Soul has been over the whole series of lives, guiding and guarding them, waiting only for ripeness. In this sense, there has been no injustice, nor is there any reason for the moral anguish that this doctrine misunderstood has inflicted on so many sensitive hearts. For we may be certain that these very hearts that deeply concern themselves with the problem of election, thereby prove their ripeness; that concern itself is the work and evidence of the Soul, preparing them for the final effort and sacrifice, the sacrifice of the sense of separateness.

Nor, we may reverently suppose, is it otherwise with the choice of the disciple by the Master. He who ardently longs to be chosen as a disciple, testifies by that very longing that the power of the Master is over him; the longing itself is the Master's gift, to lead him on his way homeward.

They who have understood that wisdom which is the essence of the Vedas, who strive through renunciation and union, purified in heart, all these at the time of the end gain liberation, immortal in the realm of the Eternal.

Gone are the thrice five parts in their places, and all the shining powers in their several shining, and all works, and the self of mental action; all have become one in the unchanging Supreme.

As rivers, flowing to the ocean, go to their setting, putting off name and form, so the possessor of wisdom, freed from name and form, gains that Spirit which is higher than the highest, the Divine.

He who knows the supreme Eternal, becomes the Eternal, nor is any born in his line who knows not the Eternal. He crosses beyond sorrow, he crosses beyond sin, freed from the knots of the heart he becomes immortal.

This is declared by the Vedic verse:

They who fulfil the rites, who hear the Vedas, who are established in the Eternal, who offer themselves with faith in the one Seer; to them let him declare wisdom, who have duly fulfilled the head vow.

This is the truth which the seer Angiras declared of old. He receives it not, who has not fulfilled the vow.

Obeisance to the supreme Seers!

Obeisance to the supreme Seers!

Two phrases in this beautiful passage call for a slight elucidation. The "thrice five powers in their places" are the five senses or powers of perception, the five powers of action and the five energies which are called the life-breaths. These, with the self of mental action, make up the lower personality, and are left behind when full liberation is attained.

The "head vow" is referred by the Sanskrit commentators to a vow to carry fire on one's head as a penance or a trial of faith. But we may surmise that this vow itself is a symbol, perhaps of purification of thought by the fire of wisdom; perhaps of the resulting revival of long dormant perceptive powers. It is said, in another Upanishad, that in the head is the home of Indra, ruler of the gods. It is possible that the vow may have some relation to this.

The last sentences pick up the thread of the opening passages of this Upanishad, in which we are told that it embodies the teaching of the Master Angiras, who received it through the succession of the supreme Seers.

Moonduk Opunishud

Translated by Raja Ram Mohun Roy

Bruhma, the greatest of celestial deities, and executive creator and preserver of the world, came into form; he instructed Uthurvu, his eldest son, in the knowledge respecting the Supreme Being, on which all sciences rest. Uthurvu communicated formerly to Ungir what Bruhma taught him: Ungir imparted the same knowledge to one of the descendants of Bhurud-waju, *called* Sutyuvahu, who conveyed the doctrine so handed down to Ungirus. Shounuku, a wealthy householder, having in the prescribed manner approached Ungirus, asked, Is there any being by whose knowledge alone the whole universe may be *immediately* known? He (Ungirus) then replied: Those who have a thorough knowledge of the Veds, say that it should be understood that there are two sorts of knowledge, one superior, and the other inferior. There are the Rig-ved, Ujoor-ved, Samuved, and Uthuruvuved, and also *their subordinate parts, consisting of* Shiksha or a treatise on pronunciation, Kulpu or the science that teaches the details of rites according to the different branches of the Veds, Vyakurun or grammar, Nirooktu or explanation of the peculiar terms of the Veds, Ch'hundus or prosody, and Jyotish or astronomy: *which all* belong to the inferior kind of knowledge. Now the superior kind *is conveyed by the Opunishuds and* is that through which absorption into the eternal Supreme Being may be obtained. That Supreme Being, *who is the subject of the superior learning*, is beyond the apprehension of the senses, and out of the reach of the corporeal organs of action, and is without origin, colour, or magnitude and has neither eye nor ear, nor has he hand or foot. He is everlasting, all-pervading, omnipresent, absolutely incorporeal, unchangeable, and it is he whom wise men consider as the origin of the universe. In the same way as the cobweb is created and absorbed by the spider *independently of exterior origin*, as vegetables proceed from the earth, and hair and nails from animate creatures, so the Universe is produced by the eternal Supreme Being.

From his omniscience the Supreme Being resolves to create the Universe. Then nature, *the apparent cause of the world*, is produced by him. From her the prior operating sensitive particle of the world, styled Bruhma, the source of the faculties, proceeds. *From the faculties* the five elements *are produced; thence spring* the *seven* divisions of the world, whereon ceremonial rites, with their consequences, are brought forth. By him who knows all things, collectively and distinctly, whose knowledge and will are the only means of all his actions, Bruhma, name, and form, and all that vegetates are produced.

End of the first Section of the 1st Moondukum.

Those rites, the prescription of which wise men, *such as Vushisthu, and others* found in the Veds, are truly the means *of producing good consequences*. They have been performed in various manners by three sects among Brahmuns, *namely, Udhuryoo, or those who are well versed in the Ujoor-ved; Oodgata, or the sect who know thoroughly the Samu-ved; and Hota, those Bruhmuns that have a perfect knowledge of the Rig-ved.* You all continue to perform them, as long as you feel a desire to enjoy gratifications attainable from them. This practice of performing rites is the way which leads you to the benefits you expect to derive from your works.

Fire being augmented when its flame waves, *the observer of rites* shall offer oblations to deities in the middle of the waving flame.

If observance of the sacred fire be not attended with the rites required to be performed on the days of new and full moon, and during the four months of the rains, and in the autumn and spring; and be also not attended with hospitality and due regard to time or the worship of Vyshwudevu, and be fulfilled without regard to prescribed forms, it will deprive the worshipper of the enjoyments which he might otherwise expect in his seven future mansions.

Kalec, Kuralee, Munojuvá, Soolohitá, Soodhoomruvurná, Sphoolinginee, Vishwuroochee, are the *seven names of the* seven waving points of the flame.

He who offers oblations at the prescribed time in those illuminating and waving points of fire, is carried by the oblations so offered through the rays of the Sun to the Heaven where Indru, prince of the celestial gods, reigns. The illuminating oblations, while carrying the observer of rites through the rays of the Sun, *invite him* to heaven, *saying,* "Come in! come in!" and entertaining him with pleasing conversation, and treating him with veneration, say to him, "This is the summit of the heavens, the fruit of your good works."

The eighteen members of rites and sacrifices, *void of the true knowledge,* are infirm and perishable. Those ignorant persons who consider them as the source of real bliss, shall, after the enjoyment of future gratification, undergo transmigrations. Those fools who, immersed in ignorance, *that is, the foolish practice of rites,* consider themselves to be wise and learned, wander about, repeatedly subjecting themselves to *birth, disease, death, and other* pains, like blind men when guided by a blind *man.*

Engaged in various manners of rites and sacrifices, the ignorant are sure of obtaining their objects: but as the observers of such rites, from their excessive desire of fruition, remain destitute of a knowledge of God, they, afflicted with sorrows, descend to this world after the time of their celestial gratification is expired. Those complete fools believe, that the rites prescribed by the Veds in performing sacrifices, and those laid down by the Smrities at the digging of wells and other pious liberal actions, are the most beneficial, and have no idea that a knowledge *of, and faith in God,* are the only true sources of bliss. They, after death, having enjoyed the consequence of such rites on the summit of heaven, transmigrate in the human form, or in that of inferior animals, or of plants.

Mendicants and hermits, who residing in forests, live upon alms, as well as *householders* possessed of a portion of wisdom, practising religious austerities, the worship of Brahma and others, and exercising a control over the senses, freed from sins, ascend through the northern path to the highest part of heaven, where the immortal Brahma, who is coeval with the world, assumes *his supremacy.*

Having taken into serious consideration the perishable nature of all objects *within the world*, which are acquirable from human works, a Brahmun shall cease to desire them; reflecting within himself, that nothing *which is obtained through perishable means* can be expected to be eternal: hence what use of rites? He then, with a view to acquire a knowledge of superior learning, shall proceed, with a load of wood in his hand, to a spiritual teacher who is versed in the doctrines of the Veds and has firm faith in God. The wise teacher shall properly instruct his pupil so devoted to him, freed from the importunities of external senses, and possessed of tranquillity of mind, in the knowledge through which he may know the eternal Supreme Being.

End of the first Moondukum.

He, *the subject of the superior knowledge*, alone is true. As from a blazing fire thousands of sparks of the same nature proceed, so from the eternal Supreme Being (O beloved pupil) various souls come forth, and again they return into him. He is immortal and without form or figure, omnipresent, pervading external and internal objects, unborn, without breath or individual mind, pure and superior to eminently exalted nature.

From him the first sensitive particle, or the seed of the universe, individual intellect, all the senses and their *objects*, also vacuum, air, light, water, and the earth which contains all things, proceed.

Heaven is his head, and the sun and moon are his eyes; space is his ears, the celebrated Veds are his speech; air is his breath, the world is his intellect, and the earth is his feet; *for* he is the soul of the whole universe.

By him the sky, which is illuminated by the sun, *is produced*; clouds, which have their origin from the effects of the moon, *accumulating them in the sky*, bring forth vegetables in the earth; *man imparts the essence drawn from these vegetables*, to woman; *then through the combination of such physical causes*, numerous offspring come forth from the omnipresent Supreme Being.

From him all the texts of the Veds, consisting of verses, musical compositions, and prose, proceed; *in like manner by him* are produced Deeksha or certain preliminary ceremonies, and sacrifices, without sacrificial posts or with them; *fees* lastly offered in sacrifices, time, and the principal person who institutes the performance of sacrifices and defrays their expenses; as well as future mansions, where the moon effects purification and where the sun *shines*. By him gods of several descriptions, all celestial beings subordinate to those gods, mankind, animals, birds, both breath and peditum, wheat and barley, austerity, conviction, truth, duties of ascetics, and *rules* for conducting human life, were created. From him seven individual senses within the head proceed, as well as their seven respective inclinations towards their objects, their seven objects, and ideas acquired through them, and their seven organs (*two eyes, two ears, the two passages of nose and mouth*), in which those senses are situated in every living creature, and which never cease to act except at the time of sleep.

From him, oceans and all mountains proceed, and various rivers flow: all vegetables, tastes, (*consisting of sweet, salt, pungent, bitter. sour, and astringent*) united with which the visible elementary substance encloses the corpuscle situate in the heart. The Supreme existence is himself all—rites as well as their rewards. He therefore is the Supreme and Immortal. He who knows him (O beloved pupil) as residing in, the hearts *of all animate beings*, disentangles the knot: of ignorance in this world.

End of the first section of the 2nd Moondukum.

God, as being resplendent and most proximate *to all creatures*, is styled the operator in the heart; he is great and all-sustaining; for on him rest all existences, such as those that move, those that breathe, those that twinkle, and those that do not. Such is God. You all contemplate him as the support of all objects, visible and invisible, the chief end *of human pursuit*. He surpasses all human understanding, and is the most pre-eminent. He, who irradiates *the sun and other bodies*, who is smaller than an atom, larger *than the world*, and in whom is the abode of all the divisions of the universe, and of all their inhabitants, is the eternal God, the origin of breath, speech, and intellect, as well *as of all the senses*. He, *the origin of all the senses*, the true and unchangeable Supreme Being, should be meditated upon; and do thou (O beloved pupil) apply constantly thy mind to him. Seizing the bow found in the Opunishuds, the strongest of weapons, man shall draw the arrow (*of the soul*), sharpened by the constant application of mind to God. Do thou (O pupil), *being in the same practice*, withdrawing all *the senses from worldly objects*, through the mind directed towards the Supreme Being, hit the mark which is the eternal God. The word Om, *signifying God*, is represented as the bow, the soul as the arrow, and the Supreme Being as its aim, which a man of steady mind should hit: he then shall be united to God as the arrow to its mark. In God, heaven, earth, and space reside, and also intellect, with breath and all the senses. Do you strive to know solely the ONE Supreme Being, and forsake all other discourse; because this (*a true knowledge respecting God*) is the only way to eternal beatitude. The veins of the body are inserted into the heart, like the radius of a wheel into its nave. There the Supreme Being, as the origin of the notion of individuality, and of its various circumstances, resides; Him, through the help of Om, you all contemplate. Blessed be ye in crossing over the ocean of dark ignorance to absorption into God. He who knows the universe collectively, distinctively, whose majesty is fully evident in the world, operates within the space of the heart, his luminous abode.

He is perceptible only by intellect; and removes the breath and corpuscle, *in which the soul resides*, from one substance to another: supporting intellectual faculties, he is seated in the heart. Wise men acquire a knowledge of him, who shines eternal, and the source of all happiness, through the pure knowledge *conveyed to them by the Veds and by spiritual fathers*. God, who is all in all, being known to man as the origin of intellect and self-consciousness, every desire of the mind ceases, all doubts are removed, and effects of the good or evil actions committed, now or in preceding shapes, are totally annihilated. The Supreme Being, free from stain, devoid of figure or form, and entirely pure, the light of all lights, resides in the heart, his resplendently excellent seat: those *discriminating* men, who know him *as the origin of intellect and of self-consciousness*, are possessed of the real notion of God. Neither the sun nor the moon, nor yet the stars, can throw light on God: even the illuminating lightning can not throw light upon him, much less can limited fire give him light: but they all imitate him, and all borrow their light from him. God alone is immortal: he extends before, behind, to the right, to the left, beneath and above. He is the Supreme, and All-in-all.

End of the Second Moondukum.

Two birds (*meaning God and the soul*) cohabitant and co-essential, reside unitedly in one tree, *which is the body*. One of them (*the soul*) consumes the variously tasted fruits of its actions; but the other (God), without partaking of them, witnesses *all events*.

The soul so pressed down in the body, being deluded with ignorance, grieves at its own insufficiency; but when it perceives its cohabitant, the adorable Lord *of the Universe*, [4] the origin of itself, and his glory, it feels relieved from grief and infatuation. When a wise man perceives the resplendent God, the Creator and Lord *of the Universe* and the omnipresent prime Cause, he then, abandoning the consequences of good and evil works, becomes perfect, and obtains entire absorption. A wise man knowing God as perspicuously residing in all creatures, forsakes all idea of duality; *being convinced that there is only one real Existence, which is God.* He then directs all his senses towards God alone, the origin of self-consciousness, and on him exclusively he places his love, abstracting at the same time his mind from all wordly objects by constantly applying it to God: the persons so devoted is reckoned the most perfect among the votaries of the Deity. Through strict veracity, the uniform direction of mind and senses, and through notions acquired from spiritual teachers, as well as by abstinence from sexual indulgence, man should approach God, who, full of splendour and perfection, works in the heart; and to whom only the votaries freed from passion and desire can approximate.

He who practises veracity prospers, and not he who speaks untruths: the way to eternal beatitude is open to him who without omission speaketh truth. This is that way through which the saints, extricated from all desires, proceed to the Supreme Existence, the consequence of .the observance of truth. He is great and incomprehensible by the senses, and consequently his nature is beyond human conception. He, though more subtle than vacuum itself, shines in various ways—*From those who do not know him*, he is at a greater distance than the limits of space, and *to those who acquire a knowledge of him*, he is most proximate; and while residing in animate creatures, he is perceived obscurely *by those who apply their thoughts to him*. He is not perceptible by vision, nor is he describable by means of speech: neither can he be the object of any of the other organs of sense; nor can he be conceived by the help of austerities or religious rites: but a person whose mind is purified by the light of true knowledge, through incessant contemplation, perceives him, the most pure God. Such is the invisible Supreme Being: he should be observed in the heart, wherein breath, consisting of five species, rests. The mind being perfectly freed from impurity, God who spreads over the mind and all the senses, imparts a knowledge of himself to the heart.

A pious votary of God obtains whatever division of the world and whatever desirable object he may wish to acquire *for himself or for another*: therefore any one, who is desirous of honour and advantage, should revere him.

End of the 1st section of the 3rd Moondukum.

Those wise men who, abandoning all desires, revere the devotee who has acquired a knowledge of the supreme exaltation of God, on whom the whole universe rests, and who is perfect and illuminates everywhere, will never be subjected to further birth.

He who, contemplating the various effects of objects visible or invisible, feels a desire to obtain them, shall be born again with those feelings: but the man satisfied with a knowledge of and faith in God, blessed by a total destruction of ignorance, forsakes all such desires even during his life.

A knowledge of God, *the prime Object*, is not acquirable from study of the Veds, nor through retentive memory, nor yet by continual hearing of spiritual instruction: but he who seeks to obtain a knowledge of God is gifted with it, God rendering himself conspicuous to him.

No man *deficient* in faith or discretion can obtain a knowledge of God; nor can even he who possesses wisdom mingled with the desire of fruition, gain it: but the soul of a wise man who, through firm belief, prudence, and pure understanding, not biassed by worldly desire, seeks for knowledge, will be absorbed into God.

The saints who, wise and firm, were satisfied solely with a knowledge of God, assured of the soul's divine origin, exempt from passion, and possessed of tranquillity of mind, having found God the omnipresent everywhere, have after death been absorbed into him; *even as limited extension within a jar is by its destruction united to universal space.* All the votaries who repose on God alone their firm belief, originating from a knowledge of the Vedant, and who, by forsaking religious rites, obtain purification of mind, being continually occupied in divine reflections during life, are at the time of death entirely freed from ignorance and absorbed into God. On the approach of death, the elementary parts of their body, being fifteen in number, unite with their respective origins: their corporeal faculties, *such as vision and feeling,* &c. return into their original sources, *the sun and air,* &c. The consequences of their works, together with their souls, are absorbed into the supreme and eternal Spirit, *in the same manner as the reflection of the sun in water returns to him on the removal of the water.* As all rivers flowing into the ocean disappear and lose their respective appellations and forms, so the person who has acquired a knowledge of and faith in God, freeing himself from the subjugation of figure and appellation, is absorbed into the supreme, immaterial and omnipresent Existence.

He who acquires a knowledge of the Supreme Being *according to the foregoing doctrine*, shall inevitably be absorbed into him, *surmounting all the obstacles that he may have to encounter*. None of his progeny will be destitute of a true knowledge of God. He escapes from mental distress and from evil propensities; he is also relieved from the ignorance which occasions the idea of duality. This is the true doctrine inculcated throughout the foregoing texts, and which a man should impart to those who are accustomed to perform good works, conversant in the Veds, and inclined toward the acquisition of the knowledge of God, and who themselves, with due regard, offer oblations to sacred fire; and also to those who have continually practised shirobrutu, *a certain observance of the sacred fire*. This is the true divine doctrine, in which Ungirus instructed *his pupil Shounuku*, which a person not accustomed to devotion should not study.

Salutation to the knowers of God!

www.ingramcontent.com/pod-product-compliance
Lightning Source LLC
LaVergne TN
LVHW041500070426
835507LV00009B/709